Communication for International Business secrets

The experts tell all!

About the author

Rus Slater is a management consultant and trainer in the UK who has worked in many areas of industry, commerce and public service. He has managed people internationally and advised on the management of international teams for many years. He is the author of *Getting Things Done*, *People Management* and *Team Management*, also in the **business secrets** series, as well as several other management titles sold internationally in English and in translation.

Communication for International Business
secrets

William Collins
An imprint of HarperCollins*Publishers*
1 London Bridge Street
London SE1 9GF

www.WilliamCollinsBooks.com

This Collins paperback edition published in Great Britain by William Collins in 2020

First published in Great Britain in 2020 by HarperCollins*Publishers*
Published in Canada by HarperCollins*Canada*. www.harpercollins.ca
Published in Australia by HarperCollins*Australia*. www.harpercollins.au
Published in India by *HarperCollinsPublishersIndia*. www.harpercollins.co.in

1

A catalogue record for this book
is available from the British Library

ISBN 978-0-00-838988-8

Typeset by Palimpsest Book Production Limited, Falkirk, Stirlingshire
Printed and bound by CPI Group (UK) Ltd, Croydon CR0 4YY

Contents

Communication is critical, communicating intercontinentally is complex

The world is getting smaller. Most of us will probably have clients, or suppliers, in another country at some time or other.

And if we don't we'll probably belong to a business community of practice that is global. The way we communicate across these boundaries can make the difference between success and failure.

With this book you should be able to communicate effectively with colleagues, suppliers and customers who come from different cultures, speak different native languages and live in different environments to your own. The chapters are:

1 **Listen and look; seek first to understand**: with international communication there are some extra critical elements to this;

2 **Say and write:** nine simple and straightforward 'rules' to help you to get your message across to others across the seas;

3 **Technology and media:** how to make contact in order to be as effective as possible;

4 **Taking the environment into account**: this helps you to consider the differences in the working environments that exist between where you are and where they are;

5 **Netiquette**: eight **secrets** to help you to master the mouse;

6 **Intercontinental differences**: this chapter aims to try to highlight some of the major cultural differences between people from different nations, without slipping into racial stereotypes;

7 **Communicating with a remote team**: this chapter aims to distil the best practice for managing a remote team.

It is easy to cause offence if you don't understand the people you are communicating with. But if you understand them, you can be as successful as if you were communicating with your own family.

Listen
and look

Communication is a two-way process. Many books on the topic, and many people, will start addressing the issue of communication by looking at the matter of transmitting information to another party. But receiving information, and understanding the environment in which your message is received, is critically important. This is particularly vital when you are trying to get a message across to someone who doesn't speak the same language as you as their native tongue. Or someone who is in a completely different time zone or working environment. You may not be able to see each other so there may be no non-verbal cues to their real meaning. This chapter aims to help you to avoid some of the more common errors in international communication.

1.1

Listen to and for the 'prepared speech'

When people are communicating in a non-native language they often prepare far more, and are much less spontaneous, than if they were talking in their mother tongue. One common element of this is a prepared speech which they may actually read from a script or they may have rehearsed to the point of memory.

There are several ways that you can tell when someone is reciting a prepared speech:

■ They tend to plunge straight in with the minimum of 'phatic' communication.
■ They tend to speak quite quickly with few pauses or hesitations.
■ There is seldom any 'um' or 'er' in their speech.
■ The delivery tends to be quite monotone with little modulation.
■ If they are interrupted, they tend to lose the flow of what they were saying.

Listening to prepared speeches can be quite annoying for many people; the characteristics listed above don't make interesting listening

"To listen well is as powerful a means of communication and influence as to talk well"

John Marshall, Chief Justice US Supreme Court, 1801–35

and the delivery style prevents (or at least discourages) you from asking any questions. However …

A prepared speech provides the speaker with a huge amount of psychological comfort that they are making their mark on the dialogue. It gives the speaker confidence that he or she is 'present' and contributing, when they may be struggling with unfamiliar words, phrases and sentence structure. If there are others involved in the dialogue who have the same concerns, it establishes a degree of camaraderie. So if you are on the receiving end of a clearly prepared speech and you find it annoying and are concerned that it is taking up time that could be spent on more pressing matters, tough it out!

- Listen.
- Thank the speaker.
- Summarize what you heard.
- Ask if others agree, or ask what parts they agree with.
- Offer you own opinions.

This may make initial meetings a little slow but in the longer run it will pay dividends as people recognize that they can communicate with confidence in a language which to them may be foreign.

Think about more than just the message people are giving you, be considerate of their need to be listened to.

1.2

'Look' for the indicators of cultural differences

Biologically all humans may be the same but our cultures are different across the globe. When you are communicating with people from a culture different to your own you need to be constantly looking out for signs that a cultural difference may be getting in the way of the message you are trying to get across.

Consider the areas where there may be different expectations or levels of comfort:

■ **Forms of address.** The practice of using people's first or given names varies from country to country. There are also differences regarding the use of titles with family names. Try to check before you meet/talk/contact someone. If you can't find out in advance, ask at the opening of the communication.

■ **Greetings.** Culturally appropriate greetings are immensely diverse. Different cultures expect or eschew different forms of handshake, kisses and 'air-kisses' (one, two or three?), hugs and bows. The exchange of business cards at a greeting is also culturally important to many peoples but of little consequence to others – make a mistake and the whole relationship starts on the wrong foot.

■ **Physical contact**. In some cultures it is a friendly gesture to pat someone on the back or touch their arm, elbow or shoulder during a conversation. In other cultures this is seen as overly familiar or invasive, either can lead to embarrassment.

■ **Self-aggrandizement**. In many cultures self-confidence is a positive plus, but in others a more humble, self-effacing attitude is more acceptable.

■ **Taking an interest in a person's private life**. Seen as evidence of caring in some cultures, in others it is seen as prying until or unless you are well acquainted.

You will be less likely to make any cultural faux pas if you find out, in advance, about the cultural 'norms' of the people you are going to interact with.

Whether or not you do, look out for signs that you may have committed a potentially embarrassing boob:

■ Someone frowning when you wouldn't expect them to be.
■ A sudden silence immediately after you say or do something.
■ A physical reaction such as a person pulling away from you.
■ Monosyllabic answers to questions that would normally elicit more response.

Don't try to replicate the other party's cultural style; this may come over as patronizing and mimicry. Simply be aware of the differences and avoid causing embarrassment.

1.3

Check for real understanding

Over the years numerous comedy sketches and real-life anecdotes have produced belly laughs or awkward situations based upon a simple lack of understanding of cross-cultural communication. The problem is sometimes simply that one party clearly doesn't understand the other and sometimes it is due to both parties having a clear understanding but the understandings being different.

Here are some **DOs** and **DON'Ts** to help you ensure that you avoid the situation that I (and countless others) fell into:

case study In the 1980s I was a young officer in the British Army. Attached to my unit was a unit of Gurkha specialists. At the end of a briefing the team, including the Gurkha in charge, went off to join their men and get on with the tasks they had been given. Several hours later I visited the Gurkha team and found that nothing had been done at all. I asked the senior chap if he had understood

DOs
- Allow extra time to brief people who are not native speakers of your own language.
- Issue your input in short chunks.
- Get them to explain back to you their understanding of the task, situation, standard or resources after each 'chunk'.
- Allow them time to make notes – the bluntest of pencils is better than the sharpest of minds when trying to remember something you heard in a foreign language.
- Once you have finished, get them to summarize to you their understanding.

DON'Ts
- Assume that you can brief a non-native speaker in the same time that you can brief native speakers. Be aware that this may create tensions if you are briefing the two 'types' of people together.
- Ask 'closed' qualifying questions: 'OK, does everyone understand/ agree with that?' You are almost bound to get a resounding 'Yes.'
- Don't take silence to equal consent/acceptance.
- Leave it too long before you check that instructions are being carried out.

Leave nothing to chance; check that everyone has a common understanding.

his instructions, 'Yes, Sir,' he replied. So I asked if he was now able to get on with the job in hand, 'Yes, Sir,' he replied. But he didn't move to start. So I asked what the problem was. 'Yes, Sir,' he replied again. It dawned on me that he was too proud to admit that he hadn't understood the instructions and I had been too dozy to realise that I wasn't being a very good communicator.

1.4

Learn about their situation

When you are in the same office, talking to a person face to face, it is easier to understand their situation. When you are communicating with someone in a different country, it is easy to forget that their situation may be completely different to yours. This will probably have an effect on their perception of you and your message.

You may be sitting in your office in Europe or North America in the late morning. You are surrounded by colleagues sitting at their workstations in a large open-plan office. Everyone is wearing a suit and tie. The air conditioning is humming quietly in the background. You have your screen on your desk in front of you showing the latest figures. Outside the window you can see snow on the ground. You are on the phone talking to a colleague in another country. What is their environment like? Do you know?

Your colleague could be talking to you as she walks around the production facility. There could be manufacturing machinery working as she walks past. It could be 97°F and 78% humidity. She could be wearing a pair of shorts and tee shirt. It could be dark outside and 11 o'clock at night where she is; the night shift started 30 minutes ago.

The local accounts office is closed for the night and most of the management are at home in bed.

A question you may innocently ask may be impossible for her to answer for another eight hours. But her environment is so different to yours that you have no idea how much pressure that innocent question may put her under.

Take a bit of time to investigate the situation in which your international partners work, whether they are colleagues, suppliers or customers. Even people who seem to have the same type of job as you may be in a very different situation; local politics, the climate or weather, the season, the time zone and local working practices can all make for very different circumstances.

Then try to remember this each time you speak with them or send them an email or text message.

You dialled their number and they answered but it is easy to forget that they may be in a completely different environment to you.

1.5

Beware generalizations

OK, that is ironic; to start a section warning of the danger of generalizations with a generalization. This book contains plenty of generalizations; it talks about people from specific countries as if they were stereotypes. It talks about media of communication as if everyone used them in exactly the same way. Clearly that is dangerous … so beware these generalizations.

When we accept any generalization as a 'rule' we are bound to make a massive mistake somewhere down the line. This relates to generalizations about people:

■ Not all people of a particular race behave in exactly the same way; they will have been exposed to a greater or lesser degree to people from different cultures. They will base their opinions on different life experiences. They will have read and followed different 'thought-leaders'.
■ No one person from any particular race or culture can be deemed to speak for their entire nation, regardless of their position in their national hierarchy. Neither will they know what everyone else in their native country thinks about any given topic.

■ It can be deeply insulting to make assumptions based on national stereotyping; so don't.
■ Beware also generalizations regarding generations; not everyone under the age of 25 is on Facebook. And some people over 50 are.

Beware generalizations about methods of communicating:

■ Not all international phone carriers charge the same rates.
■ Calls *from* Country A *to* Country B may be charged at a different rate to calls *from* Country B *to* Country A.
■ VOIP may work brilliantly between two specific areas, but may be appallingly ineffective between two other specific areas.
■ Some people are brilliant at running virtual meetings using conference call or VOIP, other people are absolutely useless (trust me, I've 'attended' some fantastic international remote meetings and some complete wastes of time!).
■ Sometimes a phone conversation is the best way to communicate and sometimes an email is actually much, much better.
■ International call routing now means that a call can show on your phone as originating in London, but the caller may be in Lahore.

When communicating internationally it is really important to engage your brain before operating your mouth.

Say and write

Now it is time to open your mouth or put 'pen to paper'. This chapter contains nine simple and straightforward 'rules' that, if followed, should help you to get your message across to others over the seas. Some of these rules are of the 'thou shalt not' variety; things to avoid like the plague (for example, using idioms such as 'avoid like the plague').

Some of them are exhortations to consciously *do* something; such as explaining acronyms and testing readability!

Some are caveats or warnings which highlight things that you probably wouldn't need to think of when communicating with your own nationality.

2.1

KISS – Keep It Short and Simple

When you are communicating with people who are not native speakers of your own language, remember that in their heads they may have to translate every word you say. Then, once they have translated the words themselves, they have to analyse the meaning. This is not an easy process. It takes time.

Keep it short:

If I'm trying to translate what you just said, and at the same time you say something else, it can become very confusing.

I'll probably miss one thing completely.

Or I might lose both!

So when speaking, keep your interjections short. Only cover one topic per 'soundbite'.

Leave a pause for people to absorb what you have said.

Ask for confirmation that that part of the message has been understood.

"I didn't have time to write a short letter, so I wrote a long one instead" Blaise Pascal (1623-62)

This is also good practice with written communication. Try to keep texts or emails to a single screen (bearing in mind that many people read their email on a smart phone, so a 'screen' may be only 50 or 60 words).

This will take more effort on your part; it is actually easier to 'ramble' than it is to be concise, so plan enough time to think about paring your communications down for the international audience.

Keep it simple:

This isn't a matter of dumbing-down or being patronizing. However, try to use simpler words rather than longer or more complex ones; so for example:

Use ...	Instead of ...
Make happen	Facilitate
Lose value	Depreciation
Belief	Paradigm
Combined effect	Synergy

Short and simple is harder than long and freewheeling, but it is worth it in the long run.

2.2

Explain TLAs (Three Letter Acronyms)

Most industry sectors and organizations abound with acronyms (not necessarily *three*-letter ones). They are a useful and usually valid way of saving time when constantly referring to something that can be abbreviated. However, this can be very confusing to people who speak a different language, especially when an acronym gets further abbreviated; for instance, Bayerische Motoren Werke becomes BMW becomes 'Beemer'.

Acronyms can create confusion in several ways:

■ I heard the letters but wasn't sure it was an acronym or a word I wasn't aware of; did you say TLA or tee elay?
■ I heard the letters and know it is an acronym but I don't know what they stand for and I'm embarrassed to ask.
■ In English the acronym for the defence alliance is NATO but in French it is OTAN.
■ The acronym makes sense in your language but not in mine; for instance in English we talk about 5 a.m. or 5 p.m. These are acronyms from the Latin words *ante meridian* and *post meridian*. The Italians

don't use the Latin or the abbreviation but actually say (in Italian) *5 in the morning* or *5 in the evening*.

■ An acronym can sound like a word with a different meaning; for instance, NASA the American Space Agency and Nasser the Arabic name, or SALT the Strategic Arms Limitation Treaty and salt the chemical or foodstuff.

■ Any acronym can have numerous meanings even in the same language; the acronym SAS can mean a British military unit, a Scandinavian airline, an environmental charity for surfers or a software brand.

While the context can provide a clue as to which acronym you are using, avoiding the use of an acronym altogether simply makes it easier for the other party to understand the message … which is your aim after all.

Never use an acronym unless you KNOW (for sure) what it means.

Acronyms help people in-the-know to communicate faster. They hinder people not-in-the-know and make it slower.

2.3

Avoid idioms

idiom

('ɪdɪəm) *noun*

1 A group of words whose meaning cannot be predicted from the meanings of the constituent words, as for example (*It was raining*) *cats and dogs*
2 Linguistic usage that is natural to native speakers of a language
3 The characteristic artistic style of an individual, school or period

As native speakers we often use idioms. They can, however, be very confusing to people who are not familiar with our idiomatic phrases.

Here is an A to Z of common business idioms in English (from across the English-speaking world), check whether you use them regularly …

A. Ahead of the curve	B. Bring it on	C. Corner the market	D. Drop the ball
E. Eyes wide open	F. Foot in the door	G. Game plan	H. Hit the nail on the head
I. In the black	J. come-to-Jesus moment	K. Knock yourself out	L. Low-hanging fruit

M. Make no bones about it	N. No brainer	O. get Outta here!	P. Pink Slip or P-45
Q. Quart into a pint pot	R. Raise the bar	S. Swimlane (as a verb)	T. Think on your feet
U. Under the radar	V. Virgin territory	W. Window of opportunity	X. generation X
Y. Your guess is as good as mine	Z. Zero tolerance		

… and if you do, make sure that you are careful when communicating internationally.

Idiomatic language is confusing enough, but also be aware of the tendency to create new words that will similarly present problems for interpreters and individuals when used in international situations:

Co-opertition: a compound of co-operation and competition used as a sort of alternative to 'friendly rivalry'

Blamestorming: Having an apparently open critiquing session which is really about pointing the finger of blame at someone

Idiomatic language may feel more comfortable to the speaker but 'can confuse the Hell out of' the listener.

2.4

Beware interpretation errors

If you are using an interpreter be aware that the original words and their meaning can easily be distorted. You cannot control or take responsibility for this, but you can take responsibility for checking an interpreter's ability and rapport before making serious decisions.

Here are ten top tips when using an interpreter:

1 Do everything you can to ensure that the interpreter has a good grasp of *both* languages to be used.

2 Brief the interpreter in advance about your objective and the subject matter. Do this in person to …

3 … help the interpreter to become familiar with your manner of speech.

---

case study At the height of the Cold War, Soviet Premier Nikita Khrushchev gave a speech which celebrated communism and condemned capitalism. In a sentence regarding the USA the interpreter anglicized one particular phrase as 'We will bury you.' To Americans already nervous about nuclear war this

4 Advise the interpreter in advance about the other party; their position/understanding on the matter in hand and their level of authority.

5 Check the interpreter's existing knowledge of any specialist terminology that you might need to use or which is likely to be used by the other party when they respond.

6 Address your words to the audience, NOT the interpreter.

7 Plan for the time it will take for you to speak and then for the interpreter to interpret. Recognize that a sentence you use may consist of twenty syllables but in the interpreted language it may take seventy or eighty. Don't rush the interpreter.

8 Don't distract the situation by engaging in any private, not-for-the-audience interactions with the interpreter or your colleagues.

9 Check for comprehension regularly.

10 Allow breaks for the interpreter to rest and the audience to assimilate your content.

11 And a bonus point … don't put any jokes, puns or witticisms in your words. They hardly ever translate well!

Being a good interpreter is a great skill. But you can help your interpreter to help you.

statement was met with a pretty emotive response. A more accurate interpretation would have been, 'We will be present when you are buried.' This is a common idiom in Russian that simply means, 'We will outlast you.' Thus, an apparent threat of Armageddon was actually little more than a little bit of national pride.

2.5

Beware translation errors

When getting a written document produced in a language other than your mother tongue you must be careful.

Below is an example of an email that I received from a business in May 2015. It triggers no spelling or grammar error warnings on Word's inbuilt checkers and it scores 39.9 on a Flesch Reading Ease Score (see Secret 2.9). It appears to be written by someone with a very good grasp of the English language ...

XXXXX
YYYYYY XXXXX, CEO
Email: XXXXXXGroup@gmail.com

At XXXXXX we concoct extraordinary contemplations and invest time rationally forming them. We picked the best thoughts and grow them to their most prominent potential. An idea can possibly get to be something big, and at XXXXXX we extend the idea into a potential thought for a business.

We give organizations thoughts and answers for succeed over their competitors. XXXXXX gives organizations course alongside believability and builds the organizations potential for achievement. We give organizations a short range arrangement and a long range arrangement. The short range arrangement is to stay afloat sufficiently long to make it to our long range arrangement.

You have been exceptionally picked Rus as you have demonstrated a reputation of good. Rus you are an applicant who is prone to get this position and we will much like you to work with us. Rus, XXXXXX is new organization situated in ZZZZZZ and we would much likely need you to work with our organization starting with an occupation for 22 people.

I extraordinarily admire your time in perusing through the points of interest of this proposition. In the event that you have any further inquiries, please don't hesitate to contact us utilizing the data given above.

Sincerely
YYYYYY XXXXXX

... but not someone who has a good grasp of the way English is *spoken*. It is tortuous, repetitive, pretentious and generally unimpressive.

I'm sure that speakers of other languages have plenty of examples of documents they have been sent by native English speakers that have been poorly translated into their language.

The 'rule' should be:

After you have translated a document get it read by a native speaker of the target language BEFORE you commit to it.

2.6

Be aware of cultural/national differences between speakers of the same language

Someone once said that the British and Americans are one people divided by a common language.[1] There are several languages which are spoken as the primary tongue of more than one nation and each nation has its regional differences.

There are more Portuguese speakers in Brazil than in Portugal and Brazilian Portuguese has many differences to the Portuguese of Portugal.

Over 400,000,000 people speak Spanish as their first language while the population of Spain is only 46,000,000; again the language is not identical between Spain and the USA, Mexico or Peru.

English is spoken in over 60 countries as an official language, but there are considerable differences in the language's use. For example:

1 This is variously attributed to George Bernard Shaw, Oscar Wilde and Winston Churchill but there is no common agreement as to who said it first.

■ If an Australian wanted you to do something immediately she might tell you to do it *on the knocker*. Whereas 'knocker' has no similar meaning to a Briton, a Canadian or an American.

■ An American might tell you that his office was on the first floor of the building; a Briton would climb the stairs *up* to the first floor and then realize that the American meant that the office was on what a Briton would call the 'ground floor'.

■ A Canadian or an American would take an elevator to the top floor of the building whereas a Briton would take the lift.

If you regularly deal with people from one particular linguistic region, make an effort to learn their specific differences to your own usage.

If you have to communicate with people from different areas, try to be more aware of the possibilities for misunderstandings. Take more care to check understanding and clarify your meaning (see Secret 1.3)

Remember that just because two people speak the same language it doesn't mean that they can't misunderstand each other.

2.7

Consider accents and dialects

Language is a fascinating thing. Not only do people speak different languages, but within any single group of nationals speaking the same language, there are variations in the accents and dialects. So much so that there are international directories of dialects.

What is the difference between a 'dialect' and an 'accent'? Really it's pretty simple.

<u>Accent</u> is the way that a particular person or group of people *sound*. It's the way they pronounce individual words and the 'musicality' of their speech generally. This can range from a simple misunderstanding due to accent:

> (In a Scottish Glasgow accent) 'Ah, ma family clubbed together an' got ma Dad herpes for his birthday.'
>
> 'Herpes?'
>
> 'Aye, herpes.'
>
> 'You gave him a disease?'
>
> 'Nae, ya fool, herpes ... he's lost all his hair so we got him hairpiece.'

To an apparently 'lazy' pronunciation:

'Sorry, what is two-season broccoli?'

'No idea, I've never heard of two-season broccoli.'

'But *you* told me it was two-season broccoli.'

Pause.

'Ah, no, I said that there are two "c's" in broccoli.'

Dialect describes both a person's accent and the grammatical features of the way that person talks.

For example, a Scottish *accent* is clearly different to the 'received' pronunciation of Her Majesty Queen Elizabeth. A Scot's use of the term 'wee' to describe something small, 'aboon' to mean above or 'ahin' to mean behind are all examples of *dialect*.

These examples come solely from the British Isles but dialect is used in English across the globe. For example, in Jamaica it is common to hear the words 'a beg yah' meaning 'would you, please'; the asker is no more begging than an Englishman saying 'I beg your pardon' when he sneezes.

An Indian speaking in English may ask 'What is your good name?' if she wants to know your *full* name, there is no suggestion that you possess a bad name as well!

Beware your own accent and dialect and if in any doubt about what someone else has said ... ASK!

2.8

People's names

A person's name is something that is the foundation of their identity. It defines them as an individual. If you call someone by the wrong name, or mispronounce their name, or use it inappropriately, you run the risk of starting the entire conversation badly. Names from cultures other than our own can seem very alien and difficult to master. But we must!

Most people's names are made up of a combination of one or more 'given' names (*chosen by* the parents) and one or more 'family' names (*inherited from* the parents).

Here are some <u>general</u> conventions regarding names across the world:

■ Given name, Other Given name, Family name. E.g. Russell Philip Slater, addressed as Russell or Mr Slater. A format common in Anglophone cultures, e.g. British, American, Canadian, Australian.
■ Given name, Father's (or sometimes Mother's) name, followed by -sson for a male and -sdóttir for a female. E.g. Björk Guðmundsdóttir. Addressed as Björk, or by full name, Björk Guðmundsdóttir, not normally Ms Guðmundsdóttir. Icelandic format.
■ Given name, appropriate word(s) for son of/daughter of, Father's name. E.g. Isa bin Osman (Isa son of Osman). Addressed as Mr (or Encik Isa). Malay, southern Indian and Indonesian format.

■ Family name, Generational name,[1] Given name. E.g. Mao Ze Dong. Addressed as Mao xiān shēng (xiān shēng meaning Mr) or as Ze Dong (where a generational name exists it is polite to use it with the Given name). Chinese format.

■ Given name, Father's Family name, Mother's Family name. E.g. María-Jose Carreño Quiñones who is the daughter of Antonio Carreño Rodríguez and María Quiñones Marqués. Addressed as as Señorita Carreño, not Señorita Quiñones. Spanish format.

■ Given name, Mother's Family name, Father's Family name. Similar to no. 5 but with the parents' names reversed. Portuguese Brazilian format.

■ Given name, Father's name and appropriate word for son/daughter, Family name. E.g. Boris Nikolayevich Yeltsin (Boris, son of Nikolay, Yeltsin) and Naina Iosifovna Yeltsina (Naina, daughter of Joseph, Yeltsin). Russian format.

As said, these are some general conventions; the whole story is way too complicated to include in this short section! www.w3.org/International/questions/qa-personal-names has a more comprehensive explanation but the simple thing to do is ask!

www.behindthename.com/articles/3.php is also interesting reading on the topic.

Get a person's name right, address them as they wish to be addressed and you are halfway to establishing a decent rapport.

1 All of Chairman Mao's siblings share the same generational name of Ze.

2.9

Test 'readability'

Many people write long documents that look impressive. They use lots of long words. They write lots of long sentences. Since they wrote it, it makes sense to *them* when they read it back. However, they can be hard work for the reader. Have *you* ever read a business document, got to the end of it and thought, 'I'm not really sure that I understood that'?

There are several different tests for 'Readability'. These are proven statistical analyses of your writing. They assess whether you are likely to educate or confuse your reader. They are not targeted at readers who do not share your first language but they all work as well with this group.

Put the words 'readability test online' into a search engine and you will be presented with a range of options. Some will be free and some need a subscription.

If you use Microsoft Word, there is a readability test option included in the spell check function.

Let's consider one: the Flesch Reading Ease test. This is a good one simply because it provides a single number score. The higher the number, the easier it is to read. Roughly put the scoring matrix looks like this:

Score	Readability
90–100	Easily understood by the average 11-year-old student*
60–70	Easily understood by 13-to-15-year-old students*
0–30	Best left to university graduates*

*Note that this is readability in the students' English language mother tongue, so it is not insulting to a non-native speaking adult.

Five tips to make your writing easier for an (international) audience to understand on a single reading:

1 **Write in short sentences**. Use a fullstop and write several shorter sentences in preference to one longer one with commas or semicolons.

2 **Use shorter words**. Where possible, use words with fewer syllables. Obviously this is not always possible; if you have to use the term 'calorific value' in a document it is better to use that term than have to write a long phrase of shorter words to define it 'as the amount of heat produced by burning'.

3 **Write shorter paragraphs**. Shorter paragraphs, like shorter sentences, are generally easier to read.

4 **Use an active voice rather than a passive voice**. 'You should write short sentences and short paragraphs' rather than 'Short sentences and short paragraphs should be used.'

5 **Use a readability test!** You can use one to test an entire document or a short element of a longer one. Either way, they are a great aid to making your work more accessible.

Write it. Read it. Test it. Rewrite it. Retest it. Publish it.

Technology
and media

In the modern world there is a range of media you can use for international business communication. In this chapter we will look at the benefits and potential pitfalls of each in turn. Obviously it depends on your message and your objective whether something is a pro or a con.

Sometimes you will have a full choice of medium and on other occasions you will be restricted to only a few options due to cost, time or other local or temporary factors.

There are seven **secrets** and each is set out in the same format; this is to (hopefully) make it easier for you to compare media.

3.1

Written communications

All written communication leaves some form of record ... just remember that if you write it once it can appear a thousand times!

1 A traditional letter

Pros	Cons
a) As traditional letters become less common it has a degree of gravitas that may be beneficial	a) Can be considered very formal
b) Less likely to go into a junk folder	b) Slow to arrive
c) Highly personal (normally sent to home address)	c) No proof of receipt
d) Confidential	d) Costly in time and postage
	e) Loss of non-verbal behaviours

2 Internal memo

Pros	Cons
a) Less likely to go into a junk folder	a) Requires an internal mail service
b) Rarer than email so may have more potency	b) Potentially not confidential
c) Personal	c) Has to be written out individually
d) Can be confidential	d) Loss of non-verbal behaviours
e) Less formal than a letter	
f) Can be 'circulated'	

3 Email

Pros	Cons
a) Very fast	a) Can go to the wrong person
b) Cheap/free	b) Can be forwarded maliciously
c) Can be used to cc or bcc	c) Stays on record 'for ever'
d) Easy to respond to	d) Encourages sloppiness in spelling and grammar

e) Is often formally/legally accepted as a binding contract	e) May not be read for hours/weekends
f) Easy to add attachments	f) Can disappear into junk folder
	g) Loss of non-verbal behaviours

4 SMS text

Pros	Cons
a) Goes to the mobile so people usually get them immediately	a) 'Limited' space for the message (160 characters)
b) More confidential than emails	b) Can be seen as 'chummy' or terse
c) Easy to respond to	c) Loss of non-verbal behaviours
d) Easy to add some attachments	

5 Intranet

Pros	Cons
a) Normally under some sort of organizational control so can be slow to get stuff online	a) No guarantee the right people will see it
b) 'Confidential' from people outside the organization	b) Can get lost in a lot of other data
c) Good for getting the same message available to everyone at the same time	c) Only a one-way form of communication
	d) Loss of non-verbal behaviours

6 Website

Pros	Cons
a) Normally under greater organizational control so can be slow to get stuff online	a) Visible to everyone, including competitors
b) More likely to be censored/edited	b) No guarantee that the right people will see it
c) Good for getting the same message available to everyone at the same time	c) Can get lost in a lot of other data
	d) Only a one-way form of communication
	e) Loss of non-verbal behaviours

All written communication allows the originator time to consider and compose their message. It also allows the other party some time to compose their response. This can be a major benefit, or a major disadvantage, depending on the situation!

3.2

Face to face verbal communications

Face to face communication (shortened in the twenty-first century to the acronym F2F) is the most common form of interaction in co-located teams. When you need to communicate with someone a long way away there are challenges of distance and time commitment but there are occasions when it is still the better medium.

F2F communication	
Pros	Cons
a) Some messages are very important. They may be important *solely* to you, or to the organization, or to the recipient. It makes it clear to the recipient that you care enough to make the effort of taking a trip and devoting the time to travel and deliver the message face to face.	a) There may be considerable direct financial cost involved in travelling to meet someone. b) The travel may take two or three days out of your schedule to get to have a one-hour meeting. c) There is seldom a complete record of exactly what was said to whom.

b) Although we call it 'face to face', by meeting in person both parties can observe all the non-verbal behaviours of each other, from a handshake to a smile, from the posture you adopt to the constant glances at a watch or clock. This helps in getting the emotions across with the words.

c) You may wish for the other party to have to respond immediately to your message. Either directly to you or in terms of their actions. Your physical presence ensures that this happens.

d) If the topic is important enough to justify an F2F meeting but is also highly contentious, it may be uncomfortable for you to deliver it face to face.

e) If the situation is as in d) it may be potentially explosive to put the other party in a position of being in the same room.

f) It may be that the communication is solely one way (for example, a termination of employment which is non-negotiable). In this instance the reverse of c) may be the desired situation.

g) You will have to be prepared to 'think on your feet' rather than craft a perfect message.

All F2F communication allows/encourages an immediate response and a potential two-way dialogue. Give consideration to the desire for this and its potential consequences before deciding which medium to employ.

3.3

Using the phone

The phone is a brilliant tool that has done a great deal to revolutionize modern working practices. You can simply dial someone's number and speak to them instantly, no matter how far away they are. Thanks to the mobile or cell phone network you can do this regardless of whether they are in the office or not.

Like other communication media this is a potential double-edged sword; it has benefits and possible dangers.

Using the phone	
Pros	Cons
a) There is immediacy and a potential urgency that is provided by the phone that is not there in written communication (see case study below).	a) Calls may be made or received at inconvenient times or inappropriate times
	b) If you go to voicemail you have to quickly decide what message to leave (or even whether to leave a message) – see **one minute wonder**.
b) Phone calling is very cheap in comparison to meeting in person or sending a letter.	

case study I know one executive who still (even in 2016) doesn't read emails; his attitude is that if a matter is urgent or important people can ring him and speak to him directly. If people don't bother to phone him their

one minute wonder Before you make a call (any call) take a moment to decide what you'll do if you get the voicemail; will you leave a message at all? Will you leave a message simply asking the person to call? Or will you try to give them the gist of the communication you intended to give directly. This will save you from leaving a recorded 'waffle'.

c) If you dial the wrong number you'll know instantly, unlike a letter or email which could get lost/go to junk and not be noticed for weeks.	c) It is easy to forget on the phone that the other party may not speak your language as a mother tongue.
d) It is harder to ignore a ringing phone.	d) You cannot see non-verbal indicators or incomprehension.
e) You can use your voice's tone, pitch and volume to give emphasis which would not be possible in writing.	e) You cannot see the circumstance of the other party; they could be driving or with other people.
f) You can hear hesitation and tone pitch and volume emphases from the other party.	

Your phone can rule your life, if you let it. Or it can be a brilliant tool for immediate business communication.

issue isn't that urgent or important so he will not bother with it. To test the effect Claire Burge, CEO and founder of This Is Productivity, set her email's auto response to ask people to ring her or speak to her directly.

3.4

Video calls

Video calling can be accessed via most smartphones on the mobile network and numerous VOIP providers such as Skype. Video calling is available through many social networking sites and is suitable for use on tablets as well as desktops, laptops and phones. It is often now included as a standard feature of software so it is very accessible.

Video calls are increasingly being used for such activities as job interviews, sales meetings, progress meetings and general catch-ups, even when the participants are in the same country. The savings in terms of travel costs and time are fairly self-evident.

Using video call	
Pros	Cons
a) You can see (some of) the non-verbal behaviours of the other party.	a) You can't see the other party's whole body so you will miss quite a lot of their non-verbal behaviours.
b) They are generally quick to set up – you can often simply contact the person and go straight on with a video call.	b) They can be difficult to use if one or other party is in an open plan area; background noise and images can be distracting.

c) VOIP (as opposed to using a landline or mobile) tends to produce a better audio quality than a standard or mobile phone call.	c) Video calls use up more bandwidth than voice-only calls so they may be less effective where one party has low bandwidth capacity.
d) You can often share data and materials via the 'text chat' facility rather than having to remember to send over the documents after the call.	d) Video calling is still quite new; many people are not yet familiar with the technology and some hate to see themselves on the screen.
e) When parties are using a headset (or computer mic and speakers) they tend to be freer and more animated than when holding a phone to their ear.	

Video calls can help replicate some F2F characteristics. Used appropriately video calls are a boon to international communication.

3.5

Conference calls

Conference calling is relatively cheap and requires no special kit other than phones. Many businesses use it a lot as an alternative to face to face group meetings. But beware:

Using conference calling	
Pros	Cons
a) You can get several people's opinions and input in one call rather than in several one-to-one calls.	a) Bad meeting management can be amplified into bad conference call management
b) It is quick, cheap and easy.	b) There is a potential danger of people speaking over each other inadvertently and giving the impression of shouting someone down.
c) Most conference-calling facilities offer a recording option so you may be able to avoid note taking.	
d) The recording option also allows people who missed a call to catch up on an unedited version.	c) It is not always clear who is speaking; this can lead to misunderstandings.
	d) If some of the attendees on a conference call are co-located (i.e. sitting in the same rooms and using a conference phone) they can easily form a subgroup which excludes the remote members of the call.
e) Some recording options offer a voice-to-text transcription if you need a written record.	

Here are the top tips for successful conference calls:

1 **Encourage participation.** Ask questions (and wait for answers!), request people to speak, get others to give their opinions of other people's comments.

2 **Be aware of people's locations.** Background noise, distractions and the difference between being at home or on the road to being in an/the office. These can all cause difficulties if you are not consciously aware all the time.

3 **Use the equipment to its full capacity.** Remember the directionality of the microphone. If using a handset, remember that you will have one hand stuck to the side of your head for the duration of the call (this might make taking notes or leafing through a relevant document difficult).

4 **Get everyone in the habit of introducing themselves** *each time they speak.* This will save people from not knowing who is contributing.

5 **Be brief.** Speak in short sentences and if you need to go on for more than two or three minutes in one go, regularly check that everyone understands/agrees/is still listening/hasn't lost the will to live.

Don't translate bad meeting management into bad conference call management!

3.6

'Screen-sharing' calls

Screen-sharing goes by many names: webinar, screen-sharing, video conferencing and online meeting being just a few. Fundamentally you can have a group of people in different locations who can see, in real time, your screen and have a conversation at the same time either over a telephone line or via VOIP.

Using screen-sharing calls	
Pros	Cons
a) The ability to use a clear, present visual aid brings a potential for much clarity.	a) Everyone has to access the software, which can be problematical if your firewalls are high powered.
b) The systems usually have a feature that tells you if someone is no longer paying attention.	b) People have to do b) above up to 15 minutes in advance (first time).
c) You can have interaction verbally or by use of a text chat pane.	c) You need to make sure you want to share your screen; you may have stuff that you don't want colleagues to see.
d) You can do a quick check that people are with you by use of the 'hands-up' or 'tick' facility ('interaction tools').	d) The systems do require reasonable bandwidth so people calling in with poor broadband speeds may get a delay.
e) The visual and the audio can usually be recorded for file or sharing.	e) You still run the risk of 'Death by PowerPoint' if you don't create good slides!
f) No one needs to travel anywhere, so it is cheap and environmentally friendly.	f) Many people tried the technology when it was brand new and still prone to problems. They have not recognized the major advances in the last couple of years and so are reluctant to use it.

Here are five things to do to get the most out of online business communication:

1 **Get everyone else familiar with the technology.** Before you need to use a screen-sharing system for real, have a practice session. Get everyone to download the software, log on and have a play with it. Practise sharing slides or documents, moving from one page to another and one document to another.

2 **Check the basics.** Make sure that everyone can speak and hear everyone else.

3 **Agree some ground rules.** For instance, will we all be mute unless the chair unmutes people so they can speak, do we announce our name before speaking, can we all be on time, is everyone aware that the chair can tell if they aren't paying attention?

4 **Shut down all other applications.** Everyone should do this; they take up bandwidth and the constant pinging of people's email alerts can be heard by everyone!

5 **Switch off other electronics that may interfere.** Mobiles and tablets 'polling' for a Wi-Fi signal can cause nasty noises as interference on VOIP.

If you've never used it screen-sharing can be a bit intimidating. Planned and introduced well it can be brilliant!

Taking the environment into account

This chapter deals with the physical environment in which your colleagues are working.

It is easy, when dealing with a myriad of issues, to forget that the people you are communicating with may be in a completely different environment to the one that surrounds you. This will result in different perceptions and if these aren't taken into account then problems can arise.

4.1

Time zones and time differences

There are 24 time zones in the world. Each lies roughly along a 15-degree arc of longitude. Then it gets complicated! India and China are geographically large countries but each uses only one time zone; the time on their western borders is the same as the time on their eastern borders. Russia, however, has 11 time zones of its own and the USA has nine in total, of which five cover the contiguous states.

So what? Imagine that you are in New York and you have just got into work at 09.00 in the morning. You need some information from a colleague in Madurai so you call her or email her. In Madurai it is 6.30 in the afternoon, and she is just ending her day.

You are fresh and ready for anything.

She is shattered and ready for a break.

If she doesn't work late to get you the information you won't get it before you come in tomorrow.

If you don't realize this you may cause her a great deal of difficulty over something that is not urgent at all.

When you are arranging online meetings, conference calls or just phone discussions with people from across the globe, you have to remember that although *generally* time zones are split in whole hours, this is not always the case:

Australia is 9.5 hours ahead of GMT

Nepal is 5.25 hours ahead of GMT

Venezuela is 4.5 hours behind GMT

Then you get all the complexities of Daylight Saving Time (DST) and British Summer Time (BST). This could be simple... except that generally BST starts a week earlier than DST so though they quickly get into synchronization, for a week they are out of step with each other. And ... in the southern hemisphere the equivalent shift to 'summer time' is several months out of step with the northern hemisphere as the seasons are at different ends of the yearly calendar.

You may also be surprised to know that governments around the world quite often change the time zone of their country to suit emerging issues and challenges. You'll probably get due notice of this since you are working with people in different countries regularly but it is worth bearing it in mind!

(In Israel the Palestinian population generally works on a different time zone to the Jewish population!)

If you have a bit of spare time (about 10 minutes) there is a very good little video at www.youtube.com/watch?v=-5wpm-gesOY that debunks all the theory you may have about time being a simple matter of looking at the watch on your wrist or the screen of your smartphone or the bottom left-hand corner of your computer screen.

When speaking internationally to a colleague it is a good plan to always start the conversation with a question about the local time. It could save a lot of heartache.

4.2

Local working practices with regard to time

Virtually all humans work to a 24-hour clock.

In the industrialized West we use the phrase '9 to 5' to describe a typical working day. Not all nations have the same paradigm. Local differences may appear odd to people from other cultures but there is usually a good reason for the differences.

Here are some examples of different working practices common (but neither exclusive nor mandated) in different countries around the globe:

■ France operates a legally mandated 35-hour working week.
■ In Brazil the lunch 'hour' is more commonly two hours.
■ Smaller companies' employees in India commonly work 11-hour days, six days a week.
■ In Mediterranean Europe (and some Hispanic American countries) it is still common to work the day around a siesta; a post-lunch 'power nap'. This gives a working day that looks something like 10 a.m. until 1 p.m. and 5 p.m. until 9 p.m.

"Mad dogs and Englishmen go out in the midday sun"

Noel Coward (1899–1973)

■ Many devout Jews (regardless of their geographical location) cease work before sundown on Friday; in Northern Europe in November this could be as early as 3 p.m.

■ Practising Muslims pray five times a day. Only three of these devotions are likely to fall during 'normal' working hours but, due to international time differences, they are all worthy of consideration by non-Muslims.

Not only do people work a different working day in different cultures but different days are worked. While in America and Europe Sunday is the traditional 'day of rest' many Muslim countries, such as Bangladesh, Saudi Arabia and the United Arab Emirates, have Friday as their non-work day. Some other Muslim countries, like Pakistan, count Friday as half a rest day after the traditional Friday prayer is over.

In Russia and some other former Soviet states of Europe it is still common for people to work on Saturdays, but not at their usual place of employment and not for pay; it is common for people to volunteer in community projects (particularly manual labour) known as 'subbotniks'.

New Year's Day is a traditional public holiday across the globe but it is not always 1 January. In Afghanistan it is celebrated on 21 March and in Ethiopia it is in September. Wikipedia has a useful summary of different public holidays (not just New Year's Day) around the globe at: http://en.wikipedia.org/wiki/List_of_holidays_by_country.

It pays to think more deeply about local working practices than just 'What time is it in ... ?'

4.3

Local office facilities

Workplaces are not the same the world over. The difference between an executive's office space in New York or downtown Beijing could be massive. The difference between either of those and an office in rural England or small-town India could be even greater.

Take a moment to think about an office that is in a different country and environment to your own. For instance, if you are in a corporate HQ in downtown Manhattan, consider an office in a manufacturing facility in Madurai.[1] What common facilities would both have?

Quite probably both will have a computer linked to the Internet and both will have phones. Other than that it is quite probable that there will be nothing else that is available *in the room* in both locations:

■ The person in Madurai may be the only person in the office so has a degree of peace and privacy. The person in Manhattan is in an open-plan office alongside noisy or nosy people who do completely different jobs.

1 A thriving city in southern India with a population in excess of a million, where people are employed in IT, motorcycle manufacture, creation of rubber products (such as tyres and shoe soles), granite and chemicals.

■ Madurai probably has a dedicated printer on the same desk as the computer, whereas in Manhattan it is shared with several other workstations and is located about 45 feet away.

■ A Manhattan executive undoubtedly has the capacity to receive and send emails and access servers while on the move via a smartphone. Even a manager in Madurai *may* not have this 'luxury'.

■ Manhattan will be air-conditioned and soundproofed. Madurai may have a fan but, being attached to a manufacturing facility (and considerably closer to the Equator), may be noisy and smelly.

■ Manhattan may have a ban on drinks at the desk which means leaving the workstation for refreshment. Madurai may have a chai trolley delivering to the workforce.

■ Madurai may still use a fax machine regularly whereas the staff in Manhattan may not even remember what a fax machine looks like.

■ Manhattan may have a stationery store on the same floor whereas Madurai may have to go out to the nearest shop to buy stuff on an as-needed basis.

Please note that the use of Manhattan and Madurai is not designed to be racist or nationalistic; you could replace Manhattan with Munich and Madurai with St Mary Mead and still get the same result.

The facilities you take for granted may not be available to a contact in another country; try to remember that.

4.4

Local climatic conditions and seasons

I'm British and therefore in common with the stereotype I'm obsessed with the weather! Increasingly, in industrialized countries we are working in homogeneous air-conditioned and centrally heated environments, but the weather inside the workplace is only one part of the story.

Due to the differences in the seasons in the northern and southern hemispheres, someone in Johannesburg contacting someone in Sweden may be in a completely different environment.

They are both on the same time zone.

Both may be sitting in a climatically controlled office …

… but one may have walked to work in shirtsleeves and sunshine while the other may have had to dig the car out of a metre of snow. One may be looking out of the window at clear blue sky and people in shorts and tee shirts, the other may be looking out at the darkness lit by streetlights on snowdrifts.

Although both are at work and professional, the amount of natural daylight and the effect of bad weather on people's morale and outlook (not to mention their timekeeping or presence in the office) is well worth considering. There is a short academic article on the topic at http://psychcentral.com/blog/archives/2008/11/09/weather-can-change-your-mood/ which makes fascinating reading:

■ High humidity is a predictor for lack of vigour, elation and affection.
■ As the number of hours of sunshine increases, optimism generally increases.
■ High levels of humidity lower scores on concentration.
■ Rising temperatures lower anxiety and scepticism.
■ In the winter months, as the temperatures drop and the days grow shorter people are more likely to be affected by feelings of sadness and depression.

NB The person in Sweden is not necessarily likely to have higher anxiety and scepticism than the person in Johannesburg *due to the lower level of humidity in Scandinavia in relation to Johannesburg*. The effect is likely to be seen as local weather changes over a period.

Changes in local weather are likely to have an effect on people's attitude and capacity ... be considerate.

4.5

Local purchasing capacities

Whether you are dealing with an organizational colleague or a supplier or customer, remember that there may be significant differences in their capacity to obtain the resources that are immediately (or easily available) to you.

We are all aware that a senior manager has greater buying power and can get things faster than someone lower down the proverbial food chain. That is a universal trait. But what other factors may affect your contacts' ability to buy in the resources they need at the time they need them?

■ Consider the local *management* culture. While you may work in a flat, non-hierarchical structure, your contact may be operating under a command/control/compliance paradigm that makes it seem as if they need a director's signature to spend a penny.

Working recently with a UK-based multinational I came across this as a major issue. A small element of the UK business had been exposed as having committed some dubious working practices. The result was a clampdown on individual initiative and an imposition of a draconian governance culture. This was imposed company-wide and so affected their non-UK staff as well. It became difficult to continue to provide an agile, customer-centric service while having to rely so much on senior management 'supervision'.

■ Consider the availability of resources locally. Availability of manpower,[1] energy supply or material varies across the globe.

■ Consider local legislative restrictions on recruitment. Due to differing labour laws it is easier and quicker to recruit in some countries than others. Similarly, it is harder to lay people off in some countries than others.

■ Consider the different national norms. America uses a different default voltage to the UK. An American ton (more accurately a 'short ton') is 2000lb, different to an Imperial ton at 2,240lb, and neither equates easily to a metric tonne of 1000kg or, to be consistent, 2,204.6lb.

■ Consider local transport options and customs. That which you may be able to get on next-day delivery from your high-street supplier could be either:

- Prohibitively expensive to ship in; or
- Unavailable due to local law (for instance, many chemicals commonly available in the USA cannot be found in Europe due to Health and Safety rules); or
- Inaccessible due to the need to 'grease the palms' of officials in order to get them into the country (global organizations are increasingly preventing their executives from entering into unofficial payments under Anti Bribery & Corruption rules).

Just because you can get the resources you want to achieve, it doesn't mean that everyone else can. Remember that!

1 No sexism intended.

4.6

Local attitudes to family, friends and others

Attitudes to the 'work ethic' are not consistent across the globe. There is also some evidence that newer generations in the industrialized West have a greater commitment to family, friends and the environment than perhaps their parents or grandparents did.

Generational shift:

A 2015 report from UBS[1] found that 'Wealth is also a blessing and curse for families. While millionaires say they value family above all else, and their wealth is aimed at improving their lives, they also say they sacrificed too much time from family to make their wealth.' Millionaires' 'biggest regrets relate to mistakes they made with spouses and family members'.

Bentley University in the USA surveyed over a thousand undergraduate Generation Y millennials and found that as few as 13% wanted to become a CEO or president of a company.

1 http://www.cnbc.com/id/ 'Millionaires feel stuck on a 'treadmill': Survey'

If you look at the Organization for Economic Cooperation and Development's (OECD) Better Life Index there is a massive difference between nations' work–life balance, for example:

Denmark	9.8
Spain	9.3
Greece	7.1
United Kingdom	6.1
Poland	5.6
United States	5.3
Korea	2.5
Mexico	2.4

www.oecdbetterlifeindex.org/countries/united-kingdom/

These figures are calculated on the basis of the number of hours spent in work in comparison to the number of hours spent in leisure activities (spending time with friends, family and sleeping). They only relate to people in full-time, paid employment, so are not skewed by full-time parents who might otherwise fall between stools. Though these figures may look extreme, the Danes have on average 16.1 hours of leisure time per day and the Mexicans have 13.9.

Don't expect everyone to put in long hours – many human beings have 'got a life'!

Netiquette

We use email a lot in international communications, for many reasons.

Email is quick and easy; sadly, 'quick and easy' often results in ill-considered and slapdash.

In this chapter we will look at six ways that we can make our emails more effective for international (and domestic) addressees.

We will look at the subject line and salutations, timing and signing. We will look at the need for proof reading and read receipts. We *won't* look at length and readability; those we covered in Secrets 2.1 and 2.9.

Finally, in this chapter, we will say a word or two about social media.

5.1

Get your salutation right

The way you start the text of an email will generally set the tone in which the recipient reads it. Here are some examples of common reactions to different approaches. I've used my name, Rus Slater, here as the example to avoid upsetting anyone else.

Opening text	Probable reaction
Dear Reader….	'You don't know my name, can't be bothered to find out and you've sent this email to 200,0000 people … delete'
Hi	*If I genuinely do know you*: 'Ah an email from my friend…read on' *If I don't know you*: 'Whoa, slow down. You are not my mate and I don't kiss on a first date! … probable delete'
Dear Russell	'I don't like the name Russell which is why I use "Rus", so straight away I know I don't know you and you are trying to be chummy. I'm already unhappy! … delete'
Dear Russell Slater	1. 'I don't like the name Russell which is why I use "Rus", so straight away I know I don't know you and I'm already unhappy! …delete' 2. 'In English it is unusual to use given **and** family name (it is sometimes suggested when the writer doesn't know the recipient **and** is unsure of their gender; using the forename avoids having to use a gender-specific title) so it looks clumsy … delete'
Dear Mr Rus Slater	'In English it is very unusual to use a title **and** forename **and** family name so it looks really clumsy (to me, it suggests a poor use of mail merge) … delete'

Dear Slater	'This **was** the formal way that a social superior addressed a social inferior in Victorian England so unless you are my former commanding officer or Equerry to Her Majesty ... delete'
Rus	*If I know you and/or your email is in response to one of mine:* 'Hmmm, is this a bit terse, am I going to read something upsetting like a disagreement? ... read on a bit carefully' ... unless we usually drop the greeting so: 'Lovely to hear from you ... read on'
Hi Rus	*If I know you:* 'Great, lovely to hear from you ... read on' *If I don't know you:* 'OK you are an informal sort of person and you have made the effort to get my name right so ... read on'
Dear Jane	'You have copied and pasted an email to several people from one original but you have forgotten to change the salutation ... doesn't look very professional but I'll read on a bit'
	If I know you: 'What, no greeting ... we are "chatting" ☺ ... read on' *If I don't know you:* 'Arrgh ...Spam ... delete'

See Secret 2.8 for name protocols and orders for people from different cultures and nationalities.

The salutation is the first two or three words; upset the recipient with those and they won't read your email or they'll read it in the wrong voice (see Secret 5.7).

5.2

Prof reed you're email

It's quick and easy to send or reply to an email; mos
office based staff do it dozens of times a day. Sadly thi
means that many emails go out with simple and basi
errors for want of a tiny bit more effort in proofreading

Emails that contain spelling and grammar errors may be con
sidered as spam or a scam. Errors in the address or the subject line ca
cause emails to be halted by firewalls or simply to go to the wron
recipient. Emails full of errors or contradictions can make you lool
unprofessional or simply be ignored.

Here are six <u>basic</u> errors that people make:

1 Not checking the email address fully – forheavenscake.co.uk i
a completely different recipient to forheavenscake.com
davesmith@ is a different guy to davidsmith@ and a totall
different guy to david.smith@ who isn't david.smith123@

2 Forgetting to put in a greeting – as in the last example i
Secret 5.1

3 Not updating the subject line – when two parties simply kee
hitting 'Reply', the subject line can rapidly become completel
out-of-date. This may not create a problem but when the subjec
line and the email content are taken together it may have becom
contradictory or even a completely different message, for instance

To: Rus Slater;

Thank you Rus, how very miserable! But silver lining...it's Friday tomorrow

Kind regards,

████████

one minute wonder Check the whole email, not just the content text, read it carefully before you hit the 'send' button. Read it backwards to check spelling. Spelling check to backwards it read.

4 Words missed out altogether – I received an email that clearly stated 'Please note we will be paying travelling expenses for attendance at this event'… what was actually meant was that we will **not** be paying them. Spell check won't pick that up!

5 Misspelt words – while a spell chequer May Sea most miss takes sum thymes it won't pique up words such as the heading of this secret or this particular paragraph; they our wright words in the incorrect plaice.

6 Not signing off adequately – this may not be a problem if your email address is fully self-explanatory. However, if the email comes from info@ or sales@ or smith4253@ the recipient may be @ a loss.

Once you have sent an email, you have said it. If you didn't mean it that way, tough! So check it first.

5.3

Write 'good' subject lines

The subject line is one of two important elements that make your recipient open your email and do so in the 'right' frame of mind. The other is your email address and therefore your standing; you can't change the latter easily so we'll concentrate on what you can change ... the subject line.

Imagine you have just opened your inbox in the morning and it looks like this:

!	📎	🏷	From	Subject
	📎			Today's meeting
				Soccer
				Month End Reports
!				Fire Alarm Test: 10.15 This morning EOM

Perhaps better subject lines might be:

!	📎	🏷	From	Subject
	📎			Today's meeting 1100 agenda attached EOM
ò				Soccer; are you interested in playing 5 a side?
!				ACTION: Month End Reports; figures by Friday 0915 pls
				URGENT: FYI Fire Alarm Test: 10.15 This morning EOM

By simply adding a few words to the subject line the sender can save the recipient time and effort.

Here are five simple ways to improve subject lines for better communication:

1 Use the delivery symbols for high importance (!) and low importance (⇩) intelligently

2 Develop a series of common abbreviations for subject lines such as:

ACTION: when you need the recipient to do something

URGENT: when you need something quickly

FYI: when you are simply informing the recipient of something

SOC: for social things such as sports clubs, drinks get-togethers or jokes

REQUEST: for a request for support

EOM: end of message (This tells the recipient to not bother opening the email as there is nothing there; the whole message is in the subject line)

3 Refer to attachments in the subject line if that is all you are sending the email for

4 Keep subject lines short so they don't get truncat—

5 Never send an email without a subject line!

People do judge an email by its subject line; so make the subject line work for you.

5.4

Use the timing capacity

Many people in the modern world are almost addicted to email. They check their email 15 or 20 times a day. 39% of Americans[1] surveyed check their work email out of hours several times a day. 81% check their work email over the weekend. 59% check their work email while on holiday.

In Secrets 4.1, 4.2 and 4.6 we looked at the time differences involved in international business communications. Let's imagine that you send an email when <u>you</u> are at work but the <u>recipient</u> is now out of hours, on a weekend or even on holiday. It is likely that they will react to your email. This may seem loyal and hard working but it is also unfair and potentially dangerous. Do you want to be legally responsible for causing stress-related illnesses among your remote team?

You can draft an email and set it to send later, when the recipient(s) are back at their desk (the survey quoted above found that 6% of Americans had checked their work email while at a funeral or when they or their partner was in the act of giving birth!).

1 www.gfi.com/blog/survey-81-of-u-s-employees-check-their-work-mail-outside-work-hours/

Assuming that you have MS Outlook, this is how you do it:

■ Type your email as normal but don't hit the send button.
■ Click on the 'Options' tab and look for 'More Options'.
■ Select 'Delay Delivery'.
■ A dialogue box will appear that gives you drop downs and radio buttons for 'Settings', 'Security', 'Voting' and 'Tracking'. Check the Do not deliver before:' box and select the date and time from the drop down menus.
■ Close the box and click 'Send' in the email.

If you and the people you work with use smartphones for texts and emails there is also a capacity, either built in or as an app, for most smartphones to not notify you of incoming messages during certain times. Some of these include the capacity to automatically silence your phone when you are in a scheduled meeting and reactivate it when the meeting finishes – hands up everyone who has switched off their ringer for a meeting and forgotten to switch it back on afterwards! Find out about some of these facilities at: www.techlicious.com/how-to/how-to-make-your-Smartphone-smarter/

The technology is there to help you to time your communications more considerately, use it!

5.5

Copying and read receipts

Some emails really need to be shared. *Sometimes* you send an email and you really need to be sure that the recipient has got it. However, using the cc facility indiscriminately or asking for read receipts too frequently or inappropriately can be dangerous.

Dangers of sending ccs of your email:

■ The real recipient may be left wondering why you have copied in her boss on your email.

■ Everyone who has been copied in has to open and read an email that they don't really need: if you cc just one email a day to the whole 10-person team, 9 of them each wastes 30 seconds on it. That is four and a half minutes per day, five days a week, 50 weeks a year. That adds up to 18 hours a year.

■ People who are copied unnecessarily start to resent the waste of their time and your reputation falls.

■ People then miss the important email to them because it was lost in the flurry of timewasting cc'd emails.

■ If just one person in the team hits the 'reply all' button that 18 hours of wasted time jumps to 36 hours of wasted time.

■ Every email sent has to be stored on the server; most work email accounts have a limited storage capacity (for lots of good reasons). Every unnecessary copy takes up space.

The same dangers apply to sending your email to a group rather than specific ccs; groups can become out-of-date quickly and so waste is prevalent.

Dangers of asking for read receipts:
In Secret 2.2 we looked at TLAs. One common English language TLA is CYA. It stands for Cover Your Ass. In other words, create an audit trail that will exonerate you if things go wrong. This is a predominant reason for asking for a read receipt; so the recipient cannot deny knowledge of the content of the email in the event of an issue arising in the future.

Many people consider read receipt requests to be rude. Many take the view that, if the email is that important, picking up the phone would be better than asking for a read receipt.

Before ccing an email, hitting 'reply all' or asking for a read receipt: stop. Think. Ask yourself whether you really need to!

5.6

Use a signature block – it helps

An email signature is the equivalent of your business card – small, simple, but no less essential to your individual professional persona. Like a business card it should give the recipient *all* the information they need about who you are and how to contact you … but at the same time not be longer than the email itself!

Dos and Don'ts of email signature blocks:

Dos	Don'ts
Have a signature block	Include an enormously longwinded legal disclaimer (unless you are forced to by organizational policy)
Set it up to NOT appear on forwards and replies (strings otherwise become monstrously long)	Include images; although most servers can now deal with images often the individual recipient has to accept them which may mean your signature block is full of little icons like this
Include your name and a job title	Put any links too close together; about 50% of emails are read on smartphones or tablets … if someone can't 'thumb' a link it is useless
Include your contact details	Write more than 70 characters across for the same reason as immediately above

Here is an example of a pretty good email signature block:

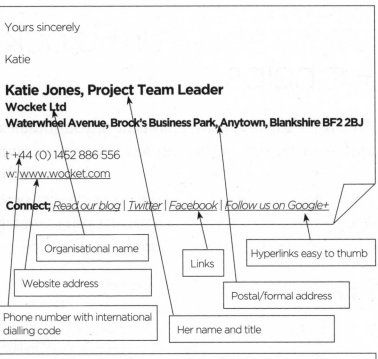

Yours sincerely

Katie

Katie Jones, Project Team Leader
Wocket Ltd
Waterwheel Avenue, Brock's Business Park, Anytown, Blankshire BF2 2BJ

t +44 (0) 1452 886 556
w: www.wocket.com

Connect; *Read our blog* | *Twitter* | *Facebook* | *Follow us on Google+*

Organisational name

Website address

Phone number with international dialling code

Links

Hyperlinks easy to thumb

Postal/formal address

Her name and title

She has used a noticeably different typeface for the main text of the email, so it stands out. There is no wordy disclaimer or environmental message. No more than 70 characters across.

Your signature block is the last thing people see but the first place they look for contact details, so make it count.

5.7

Write and read emails wisely

Emails are quickly written and quickly sent. There are no non-verbal cues in emails; no one else knows the tone of voice in the writer's head as (s)he wrote it, the recipient can't see the look on the sender's face or the volume at which the words should be read. It is easy to misconstrue the emotion behind an email.

Before you send an email:

■ After you have drafted it and before you proofread it, read it. Ask yourself if it could be read in a different tone of voice. If it can, and that would effectively change the message, then change the words.

■ Consider using emoticons. Some people and organizations believe that these symbols of digital emotion are unprofessional. However, a Dutch research team led by Daantje Derks at the Open University of the Netherlands[1] concluded that: 'emoticons can serve as non-verbal surrogates for visual cues in face to face communication and certainly have an impact on online message interpretation'.

1 www.ou.nl/Docs/Onderzoek/Definitieve%20versie%20Exploring%20the%20 Missing%20Wink.pdf

one minute wonder Don't write the subject line until you have finished checking and proofreading each email; that way if you accidentally hit send the message won't go; you'll get a reminder that the subject line is blank.

Before you reply to an email:

■ If you read an email and it annoys you, don't hit the reply button. Stop.

■ Read it again in a different tone of voice. Is the email actually as cutting/sarcastic/critical/negative/derisive/mocking/disrespectful/scornful as it seemed on first reading?

■ If it is, stop. Don't hit the reply button.

■ Wait a while (obviously 'a while' will depend on the actual content of the email).

■ Then read it again.

■ Is it still as negative?

■ If so, now is the time to act; but don't hit the reply button.

■ Email threads with rising and extreme emotions are referred to as 'flaming' and seldom end well for either party.

■ Pick up the phone. Call the sender. Stay calm and ask about the issue. Discuss it.

Avoid flaming at almost any cost ... it nearly always ends badly. And it is in writing!

5.8

Consider 'social media'

Does that title say 'social' media? Isn't this book supposed to be about 'business' communication? If so, then the topic of social media is irrelevant. Anyway, many companies' IT firewalls block access to social media because it is a distraction from actually working, so we don't need to pay any attention to social media.

WRONG!

The topic of social media and its uses in international business is massive: far too big to think of covering in one short secret. Just to get you started, though, take a look at this video on YouTube: www.youtube.com/watch?v=0eUeL3n7fDs

It is eye-opening to anyone not already really steeped in the world of social media.

Social media is becoming increasingly important in the world of business.

■ Potential customers, both business and personal consumers, search for suppliers online on social media. Many nowadays search the social media sites before or in preference to the more established search engines.

■ Prospective employers search for possible employees on social media. Many of the social media providers now have dedicated recruitment tools that are used by candidates, agencies and employers. Facebook and Twitter are not solely for 'social' purposes any more; according to a 2014 survey[1] 66% of recruiters use Facebook and 52% use Twitter.

■ Prospective employers screen potential and existing employees on social media. This can throw up many interesting anecdotes; http://time.com/money/3019899/10-facebook-twitter-mistakes-lost-job-millennials-viral/ lists a whole series of cases where social media was used for unsocial, or even anti-social, purposes.

■ People recommend or badmouth your products and services on social media. Other people, be they customers or potential customers or employees or potential employees, read and take account of these. The song 'United Breaks Guitars' has had over 15 million YouTube hits at time of writing … there is such a thing as bad publicity.

■ Savvy organizations use social media to actively respond to relevant news stories, update their customers about their products and services and generate customer loyalty.

The world of social media evolves fast; rather than try to give a set of tips on its use for international business communication here, there is just one piece of advice. It is built from the video referenced earlier in this secret:

Social Media isn't a fad – it is a fundamental shift in the way businesses communicate. It isn't a matter of whether or not you want to 'do' social media; it is whether you want to survive.

1 https://www.jobvite.com/wp-content/uploads/2014/10/Jobvite_SocialRecruiting_Survey2014.pdf

Inter-
continental
differences

International business communication crosses borders and cultures.

People from different countries, different cultures and different regions are different in more ways than simply the colour of skin and facial features. People have different traditions, different expectations and different tolerances. None is better or worse; they are just different.

Lots of hurt can be caused by being ignorant of these differences. By the same token the human race is becoming more homogeneous; the cultural differences between Japanese people and Britons are getting smaller. While this chapter highlights some of the more common differences they should not be taken as incontrovertible 'truths' about humanity's different races.

6.1

Be honest

Many organizations 'off-shore' their contact centre operations to countries where their labour costs and overheads are cheap. Fiction writer Deborah Moggach used this fact as a plot device in her book *These Foolish Things*.[1] One thing that upsets people on both sides of the debate about this is when the staff aren't honest about their names or location.

Some contact centre staff have, in the past, been instructed to:

■ Fluently speak a second language (usually English) AND
■ Lose any accent in preference for a neutral one AND
■ Then to use an anglicized name in preference to their own culture/language's given name AND
■ Then to claim 'residence' of the HQ location of their employer.

Any dishonesty to callers distorts all the good intentions. It is always better to be totally honest about who and where you are; if you are 'economical with the truth' or just downright dishonest you are almost sure to be caught out sooner or later. When this happens people will (not unreasonably) wonder how trustworthy everything else is that you have done and said during your relationship. This is not a good way to continue it!

1 Now filmed as *The Best Exotic Marigold Hotel*

If you are a manager and you are tempted to try to get your staff to speak in assumed accents and take assumed names ...don't!

Be sure your sins will find you out.

6.2

Communicating with Chinese business people

It is important to differentiate between the People's Republic of China and Taiwan; their cultures are similar but not identical. More Taiwanese Chinese people speak idiomatic English than their counterparts from the mainland.

Preparation:

■ Certain colours have specific meanings in Chinese culture, mostly negative. So keep material or presentations in black and white.
■ Learn some Chinese, the effort is usually appreciated.
■ Make sure that your business card includes your title, and one side of the business card is in Chinese.
■ Being late is an insult.

At the beginning of an interaction:

■ Nodding is used to greet somebody.
■ Always acknowledge the most senior member in a group first.
■ Chinese people should be addressed with a title and their family name. See Secret 2.8.
■ If you are given a business card, look at it before you put it aside.

> "In the midst of great joy, do not promise anyone anything. In the midst of great anger, do not answer anyone's letter" **Chinese proverb**

- When presenting your business card, do it with both hands.
- Meetings begin with small talk; don't try to get down to business immediately.

During discussions:

- Few Chinese people use their hands when speaking, and most are put off by people who do. There is not an emphasis on emotions in China so keep gestures and extreme facial expressions to a minimum.
- Negative replies are considered impolite. Instead of saying 'no', say 'maybe', even if you mean 'no'. Chinese people do the same to you.
- If a Chinese person uses a phrase such as 'This is not a serious problem', or 'This is not a big deal', it usually means it actually is.
- Expect to be asked quite intrusive questions about your age, income, title, family status and other personal topics. These can come as a shock if you come from a culture where, for instance, ageism is banned. If you do not want to give a genuine answer, give a broad answer, but give an answer.
- Avoid mentioning deadlines.
- Do not discuss business during a meal.
- Keep in mind that Chinese businesses are very family-oriented; senior people in the organization may be related.
- Chinese business culture is very relationship-oriented. Expect the process of doing business with Chinese people to be a long one. In business they build relationships first, and do business afterwards.
- Generally Chinese people expect you to leave before they do at the end of a meeting.

6.3

Communicating with Indian business people

India is a massive nation and contains a diverse population; hence these are only generalizations and should not be taken as hard and fast rules.

Starting a meeting:

■ A common greeting is to press your palms together and bow slightly, saying 'Namaste' (nah-mah-stay).

■ Shake hands only when offered.

■ Respect age and seniority; Indian staff often address their managers formally as Sir or Madam. Subordinates tend to stand up when their managers enter the room.

■ Many businesses are family-owned, so be prepared to find managers related to each other.

■ Begin business conversations with small talk. Discussing personal topics is common. Be open and friendly.

Non-verbal behaviours:

■ Use the hand with an upward palm rather than pointing at slides or people.

■ Keep your eye contact brief.

■ Standing with hands on hips can be interpreted as aggressive.

"Glory lies in the attempt to reach one's goal and not in reaching it" Mahatma Gandhi (1869–1948)

Verbally:

■ In India, staff are often expected to follow instructions of their seniors, who rarely consider suggestions or opinions of their junior staff, so beware of asking people for their opinion in front of their boss.

■ Express disagreement indirectly: 'That may be very difficult' rather than 'I can't do that.' Similarly, recognize that for many Indians 'no' is often considered insulting, even over important subjects. Consequently there can be a tendency to postpone dealing with difficulties. You may only find out about problems when it is almost (or actually) too late to do much about them.

Time management:

■ People often use people and events to schedule things rather than an absolute time: 'After I have asked my manager' or 'Before the regular meeting' rather than 'At 10.45.'

■ Appointments made early in the day are generally appreciated.

■ It is common for the employees to leave work after their managers, even if their work for the day is done; this is perceived to be evidence of a hard-working person.

6.4

Communicating with British business people

Britain used to be a very homogeneous country. More recently the population has become much more diverse and varied. Many Britons whose origins are from the former British Empire speak English with a regional British accent; you will find Sikhs with Scottish accents, black people with Welsh accents and people of Chinese descent with Liverpool accents.

■ The British still lead the world in their inability to speak languages other than English.
■ The terms 'English' and 'British' are not interchangeable. 'British' denotes someone who is from England, Scotland, Wales or Northern Ireland. 'English' refers only to people from England (almost regardless of their skin colour) and while people from England are not likely to take offence at being called 'English', a Welsh, Scots or Northern Irish person may well be offended (this may well include the Scottish-sounding Sikh and the Welsh-sounding black person).
■ Networking and relationship building are often key to long-term business success.
■ Rank is still respected and many businesspeople prefer to deal with people at their own level.

"The British nation is unique in this respect: they are the only people who like to be told how bad things are, who like to be told the worst" **Winston S. Churchill (1874-1965)**

■ An elder statesman on your team will present the aura of authority that may establish good faith for many companies.

■ British handshakes are quick and firm, not lingering or a show of physical strength.

■ Most British people no longer worry about the use of a title such as Mr or Mrs and prefer simply to be addressed by their given name. Only medical doctors, the uniformed services, the clergy and academics use their professional titles in business conversation.

■ Most British people are still masters of understatement; effusive language and wild enthusiasm are often seen as a bit American.

■ Modesty in conversation is still expected; large, public doses of self-aggrandizement breed mistrust.

■ British equality laws prevent, or at least curtail, conversations that relate directly to people's age or gender. This can also include complimenting someone on their appearance – beware!

■ Business cards are exchanged without formal ritual and a card may be put away with only a cursory glance.

■ The giving and receiving of gifts is proscribed by British Anti Bribery and Corruption laws and should be avoided if possible. Lavish entertainment often counts as a gift.

6.5

Communicating with American business people

America's position as a world power means that everyone will do business with Americans sooner or later. The USA has a very diverse population but US business culture is fairly similar across the board.

■ The USA was founded on the work ethic that good, honest, hard work is rewarded. Consequently, time is money and punctuality is highly regarded. Americans often get down to business quickly without a lot of small talk at the beginning of meetings.

■ Business cards are generally exchanged during introductions without ritual. (Alternatively, they may be exchanged when one party is leaving, again with no ritual or specific meaning.)

■ A smile is a sign of friendliness, and handshakes can be quite long and powerful. Maintain eye contact with the person you are shaking hands with.

■ Good eye contact during business conversations shows interest, sincerity and confidence.

■ Compliments are exchanged frequently and are popular conversation starters.

"It does not require many words to speak the truth"

Native American Nez Perce Chief Joseph (1840–1904)

▪ Enthusiasm and a bit of razzamatazz is generally more acceptable to Americans than to their British cousins.

▪ Sports: baseball, (American) football, basketball and golf are very popular as a conversation topic in the USA.

▪ American business language can be very idiomatic. Sports terms are common in business speech, often with the speaker unaware that they are using these idioms because they seem so natural.

▪ America is also a world leader in euphemisms and veiled speech which can confuse non-native English speakers (and non-Americans):

Assignment capsule [n.]	A clearly defined job description or task. 'Stop arguing about objectives and start handing out assignment capsuels.'

See http://www.theofficelife.com/business-jargon-dictionary-A.html for more examples.

▪ Many Americans speak only one language; they may not be sensitive to the difficulties of other individuals trying to speak English. They may speak fast or very loudly (as if this will help you understand them better).

▪ If language becomes a barrier, ask for clarification and seek understanding. If you are not totally comfortable speaking and doing business in English, hire a translator.

6.6

Communicating with German business people

Stereotypically, German products are efficient, well made and highly functional. The same goes for business communications with people in Germany. Punctuality and order are valued greatly and meetings tend to follow well-defined and efficient agendas.

Professional status is generally based on individual achievement and expertise. Germans expect other people to be similarly meritocratic; they will show interest in your academic qualifications and business record, but not your favourite football team or family connections.

Non-verbal communication:

■ A handshake may be accompanied with a slight bow. Reciprocating the nod is a good way to make a good impression.

■ Personal space is appreciated; an arm's length between people is generally expected.

■ Eye contact demonstrates attention and interest; avoiding eye contact may be interpreted as conveying the opposite message.

■ Business cards are exchanged without ritual.

"*Taten sagen mehr als Worte:*
Actions say more than words"

German proverb that means 'Get on with it!'

■ Germans often show their appreciation of a presentation or a successful meeting by rapping their knuckles against the table top.

Verbal communication:

■ When answering the phone, Germans often identify themselves by just their family name.

■ Germans are generally very straightforward; they get to the point rather quickly and expect to have targeted results at the end of a meeting.

■ They are suspicious of hyperbole, promises that sound too good to be true and displays of emotion.

■ Germans tend to focus on achieving the task in hand rather than appearing to be hard working, so do not expect to find people in the office after 5 p.m. during the week; they'll have hit their targets and gone home!

■ Beware of calling people at home after 10 p.m. if you have not asked them first if it is all right.

■ Appointments are mandatory and should be made a reasonable amount of time in advance.

■ The German trait for order and discipline means a good deal of written communication, both to support decisions and to maintain records. Always remember that an email is a business letter, in which salutations and greetings should be included.

■ Make sure your printed material is available in both English and German as a sign of respect.

6.7

Communicating with Japanese business people

Japanese business protocol is quite formal; respect it and make an effort to fit in and you can get on.

■ Business cards should be printed in your own language on one side and Japanese on the other.

■ Always be early for meetings or appointments as being late is considered insulting.

■ Address a person by their last name followed by the word '*san*', which means Mr, Mrs or Ms. The Japanese prefer to use this form of address in business. It is best not to request that Japanese colleagues or contacts call you by your first name only.

■ Business cards are called *meishi* and the Japanese give and receive meishi with both hands; it is respectful to reciprocate. Present the card with your home country language side up. Business cannot begin until the meishi exchange process is complete.

■ Bows are used for greetings and farewells. They also express appreciation, accompany apologies and requests, and also convey respect.

■ It is polite to speak first to the eldest person in a group.

■ You may be asked personal questions concerning your salary, education and family life. If you do not want to answer genuinely, remain polite and try to offer a bland answer.

"*Nanakorobi yaoki*", literally 'Fall seven times and stand up eight', meaning: 'If at first you don't succeed, try again' Japanese proverb

■ In Japan saying 'I'm sorry' is a form of punctuation of politeness; for instance, Japanese people often apologize for being late, even when they are not late. You should reciprocate.

■ It is considered inappropriate to show anger, be grumpy or express negative emotions to business counterparts.

■ If a meeting becomes difficult the Japanese will often resort to silence. This is to allow people to move away from the difficult topic. Unfortunately for many non-Japanese people the 'solution' to silence is to talk more about the topic in hand; which will create even more tension > more silence > more one-sided talk > more tension.

■ While gifts are acceptable to Japanese business culture, beware of giving gifts in odd numbers. Also avoid giving sets of four of anything or anything with the number four, as these are both considered bad form.

■ Decisions are usually made by consensus. An outsider must be accepted into the group before they can have any influence on decision-making.

6.8

Communicating with Russian business people

Doing business in Russia is interesting. Russians like to gain concessions and this means that negotiations can be lengthy affairs of grinding you down. Compromising quickly can be seen as a sign of weakness, so if you concede on one thing, barter for a concession in return. Don't be surprised by a bit of theatre; loss of tempers, walkouts, threats to end the deal, and similar incidents. It's all part of the Russian negotiating policy.

■ Consider having one side of your business card translated into Russian and be sure to include your title and qualifications.
■ Generally Russians are not impressed by special visuals, flashy Power-Point presentations and the like. Stick to facts, knowledge, professionalism and expertise.
■ First meetings are often simply to assess your credibility. Be firm and dignified, while maintaining an air of warmth and approachability, but don't expect to make deals.

"To ask is no sin and to be refused is no calamity" Russian proverb

■ Always be punctual, but it is not unknown for Russian business people to turn up late. This will give a good indication of how seriously they are taking you and your proposal.

■ Russians go in for very firm handshakes. It is appropriate to refer to people by either '*gaspodin*' (Mr) or '*gaspazhah*' (Mrs, Ms or Miss) plus his or her family name.

■ Eye contact during the introduction is very important, and must be maintained as long as the individual is addressing you.

■ Mentioning Russian culture and history can be an appreciated gesture. Russians generally have a great affection for children so photos and discussion about yours and theirs can be an effective way of building good will.

■ The business dinner is often a time for 'sealing' a deal, but be aware that Russia is a drinking culture. Refusing to drink can be insulting unless you give a good justification. It is acceptable to pretend that you are drinking, but every time you empty your glass, it is likely to be refilled.

Communicating with a remote team

In this chapter we concern ourselves with your own team that is spread across the globe.

They may be all your own countrymen and women, or they may be a mix of expatriates and locally employed people. It is vitally important that absence makes the heart grow fonder rather than that they are out of sight, out of mind and out on a limb.

7.1

Have a communication plan

Critical communication should follow a plan, rather than simply be expected to happen by chance or intuition.

A clear, consensual and commonly understood communications management plan will help to set clear expectations and to provide appropriate information back and forth between team members and you as the team leader.

A good communications plan should outline:

For formal communication:

■ Who needs to be communicated with. Not everyone will need to know everything that happens within the team but some stuff is good to share for the feeling of inclusivity it brings. Your communication plan therefore needs to specify any subgroups or special sections of the team who need or don't need to be copied in.

■ How frequently. You may have a regular email update and a regular online meeting but you need to agree how often these should take place: daily, weekly, monthly or whenever.

■ The intention of the communication. Is feedback expected (from either party) or is some communication purely FYI? Why does this matter? Let's say that one person sends out a regular FYI update but people assume that *some* response is required … instead of one simple email you might, with a team of ten, get ten responses. If some of those people hit 'reply all' you could end up with a hundred emails flying around. If each of your team members also gets communication from their in-country team their inbox will rapidly fill up and their day will be spent just dealing with emails! (See Secret 5.5 for more information.)

■ Where it originates. In some cultures (see the previous chapter) staff don't initiate action, they respond to their boss. Make it clear who should be initiating what type of communication.

■ Communication medium. You probably have a choice of landline, mobile, fax, SMS texts, email, web-chat and social media. Important messages should be backed up: e.g. send a text to alert people to expect an email and contact if it doesn't arrive.

■ Actual timing of communication (to take into account people in different time zones).

For informal communication:

It is well worth trying to get people in different countries to form a team spirit and this is usually fostered by informal communication. This can be shared interests, family, holiday snaps, general chit-chat. If not openly discussed and agreed some people may be uncomfortable getting involved in this very useful activity. So make it explicit and include it in the plan. Specify the time of day, whether all inform or one-to-one, txt spk or proper language (what language), use of emoticons (☺☹).

As the manager you should take into account (i.e. consult with) the preferences of the team members, but in the end you must be responsible for the plan.

Getting the team to give their input and preferences for a communications plan is a good way to kick off team communication and planning.

7.2

Create and maintain a virtual presence

When a team all work in one place it is easy for the team leader to have a 'presence'. When the team is scattered across the country, continent or globe, it is harder to have a virtual presence. Harder but not impossible.

'Out of sight and out of mind' is a common human attitude that works against you trying to manage at a distance. Your challenge is to be visible and present, yet not in such a way that you appear oppressive or untrusting.

Here are six great ways to create and maintain an appropriate virtual presence:

1 Understand your own image; take some time to assess:

- How your voice sounds over the phone: are you clear or a bit 'blurred', are you naturally loud or quiet, do you chat or cut-to-the-chase? Do you listen?
- How your emails and texts read to the recipient; are they blunt or a bit rambling?
- Are you articulate or do you confuse?
- Are you concise or do you fill your communiques with fluff?

2 Make it a policy to speak to everyone regularly (and fairly frequently) about progress. Not just their progress; this can look like checking up on them, but about your progress and their colleagues' progress.

3 If possible use video call so your people can see your face as well as hear your voice. If this isn't possible get the team to each share a photo of themselves to use as avatars on their mobiles or VOIP call facilities. On virtual team meetings over the web use slides of these photos to accompany people giving their progress reports.

4 Delegate as much as you reasonably can (see Secret 7.8 for one way you can do this). Delegation gives you extra opportunities to create and maintain a virtual presence as you check people have the skill and motivation to take on a task and coach them through its completion.

5 Share information and ask for feedback. If you are in head office and there is stuff happening, whether it is likely to directly affect team members thousands of miles away or not, share it with them. Ask their opinions. Discuss it. This is good practice for people to feel engaged and it also gives you the opportunity to raise your profile with your team.

6 Seek feedback about your management style and their perceptions of how you could support them to do their job better.

Virtual presence is critical; too much and you are Big Brother, too little and they forget who you are!

7.3

Use the technology to replicate the communication of an F2F team

You can use all types of media in different ways to support the communication in a remote team:

Medium of communication	Good for	Comments
Landline phone call	1:1, individual or confidential conversations. You know where they are.	Relies on the person being at the geographical location of their phone.
Conference call	Getting the same verbal message to several people at the same time.	Lacks the capacity for sharing documents or visuals. Though you know someone has joined the call, they may leave without hanging up and you may be unaware.
Mobile call	Getting hold of people quickly. Anything urgent. 1:1, individual or confidential calls.	You could be talking to them while driving or in some other inappropriate situation. Can be abused thoughtlessly out of hours.

1:1 video call	Personalizing a 1:1 conversation. Interviewing, performance, management discussions.	Can be made over the net or via a mobile network. Still relatively uncommon for business calls but increasing.
Text message	Getting a short message to either a group or a single person quickly. Anything urgent but not requiring a response. 1:1, individual or confidential calls. Having a record of having sent a message. Giving people a 'heads-up' out of working hours.	Keep it short. Remember that there is a record. Really useful if you have a quick message to get to a chatterbox; you sidestep the long conversation.
Fax, email and letter	*These are legitimate forms of communication but since they don't replicate the communications of a face to face team they are not covered here.*	
Online meeting software	Holding whole team meetings or subteam meetings. (See Secret 7.6 for tips on making virtual meetings work.)	You can share your documents and allow other people to share theirs. You can use voting (polling) on the meeting. You can see if people are using other applications during the meeting. You may be able to see the other people on video. Can be minuted electronically.
Chat-room-type of method	Instant chat and discussions when people can't speak.	

The route to success is to use the appropriate medium for the message, the time and the parties concerned. Sending emails out of hours may convey unwanted hidden messages that a quick phone conversation could avoid. A text message that simply says 'Hi, how's it going?' takes seconds and shows that you care and are accessible.

Pick your media with care; often the media carries as much meaning as the message.

7.4

Be a good host

Secret 7.2 was all about the work schedule and people's job performance. Being a good host is about helping the team through more social activities but still in work time.

A co-located team lunches together and meets at the water-cooler. They know when a colleague is on holiday or off sick and they probably know each other's spouses or partners. They can have an informal business relationship easily. This greases the wheels of the team; people support each other, they have a mate to turn to for advice or a friendly word. It is a 'good thing'.

You need to create the same kind of thing in a remote team.

Arrange regular activities that have nothing to do with the team's or individuals' targets but aim to build some esprit; for example:

■ Share a virtual office tour: You're already using technology to do your work, why not use it to bond your team? Give your fellow teammates a tour of your office, using a tablet or mobile webcam. Have a walk around your workspace; show off your desk, show off the area the office is in. Then have them do the same.

■ Have a 1:1 virtual gossip: Make a point of calling one team member a day (or a week) to talk only about non-work matters. Chat about movies, your weekend, or their upcoming holiday plans. Take an interest in their life without being intrusive. Share your life. Get to

> **"We must all hang together or most assuredly we shall hang separately"** Benjamin Franklin (1706–90)

know them as people as well as team members on the other end of a phone.

■ Host a virtual happy hour: If you can get around any time zone differences create a fixed break time for all your team members to gather and gossip together over the Internet or a conference call. Set a theme for discussion: one manager hosted a Hawaiian virtual break over WebEx and had a scrolling photo album of beach scenes. People wore Hawaiian shirts and shared their pictures as well. Get people to bring a drink or meal to the event – due to time differences one person may be having afternoon tea while others are having breakfast.

■ Go social: Assuming your firewalls don't block them, make use of social networking platforms Facebook, LinkedIn and so on. Make clear that this is for non-work-related discussions to encourage light chats and sharing of personal comments.

People should be allowed to choose their friends, but with a remote team you still have a responsibility to give them the chance to get to know each other over the miles.

7.5

'Slow down to speed up!'

That title seems contradictory, but there is logic to it. When you are co-located with your people you usually can see when someone has misunderstood an instruction or is 'doing it wrong'. When they are 4000 miles away you often don't find out until they reach the deadline and produce something unacceptable.

'Slow down to speed up' simply means taking the time to ensure that people really know what is expected and know how to achieve it. This also gives you confidence that they are really on the road to success even though you can't see them. This in turn saves you time checking and them the angst of being checked up on.

■ Make sure that you really give instructions well at the outset. Follow the SMART acronym: be Specific, explain the Metrics that will be used to assess success, actively get their Agreement that they have the Ability to Achieve, ensure they understand the Relevance of the task to the bigger picture, and be doubly clear about the Time limits (bearing in mind different time zones).

one minute wonder According to a 2014 study, the three most powerful motivators are Mastery, Autonomy and Purpose. Following the advice on these pages should give your team members each one of these in large doses. That will motivate them and make your life a lot easier.

■ Before they start get them to summarize the objective and their proposed ways of achieving it. Ask them to identify the challenges they will face and the solutions they will use to overcome these.

■ Clearly set out the reporting you need from them to help you provide the support that you should.

■ The team member is now responsible for informing you of any potential issues that may affect his or her ability to fulfil those expectations. If one of those issues is their workload from their in-country colleagues then there may be a responsibility back to you to help to smooth those issues at a higher level of authority.

■ It is also your responsibility to ensure that other members of the virtual team are aware of the delegated responsibility, not only where it may impact directly on them, but also for the purpose of furthering a sense of team spirit by simply knowing what others are doing.

■ This takes time and effort (slow down) but it will make things quicker and less painful in the long run (speed up).

Then you should be able to sit back and let them get on with it.

Avoid the temptation to want action quickly; take the time and make the effort to set the foundations – then it will all run smoothly.

7.6

Run good virtual team meetings

There are a few particular practices that apply and become important when running virtual team meetings.

F2F Meeting	Virtual meeting
a) Everyone is in the same room	a) Most of the attendees are physically alone
b) As people arrive they tend to interact one on one socially until the meeting starts	b) Any social interaction is public and only one conversation can take place at once
c) People can see each other; they can read the 'body language'	c) People can't see each other so can't read each other's body language
d) Private conversations can take place but can be seen by all	d) Private conversations may not be obvious when people have their microphone muted
e) It is quite obvious if someone is texting or checking their emails as they can be seen	e) People's attention can wander to texting, emailing or just doing something else
f) Everyone is subject to the same climate and distractions	f) Different people have different distractions

The virtual team meeting principle is to create, increase and force engagement and interactions from all team members frequently; this makes it easier for everyone to focus on the meeting. In my experience it also makes meetings generally more focused and therefore quicker and more effective.

Here are some techniques that will help in achieving more interaction and engagement on virtual team meetings:

■ No long monologues: no one (and that includes the meeting chair) speaks for more than two minutes without interaction from others.

■ Ask questions frequently; get answers by the hands-up button or the ☒ and ☑ buttons, a poll, or verbally; by going 'around the room' … but get answers!

■ Verify and validate that everyone heard you or another team member who was speaking.

■ Call on people by names, and get everyone to answer with names (similar to radio chatter where people use their call-sign with each interaction).

■ Let people know that the technology lets you see if someone opens another application (such as their email) … then if you see the '!' symbol appear initiate an interaction with that person.

■ If possible use live video on meetings, if not possible (due to bandwidth) have photos of the people so everyone gets to know their faces as well as their voices.

■ Keep track of who spoke on what topic and when; refer to this in the discussion.

■ Long explanations should be written down and sent out ahead of time.

■ Speak slowly, use short sentences, be concise and avoid slang and cultural references.

■ Make the implicit explicit; describe and state what seems obvious; examples are: in this country we will be closed on Monday for a holiday; a snow storm here may cause power outages this week.

Virtual meetings, run well, can be focused, interactive and very effective. People will love to attend them. Especially since they can do so in their pyjamas!

7.7

Communicate with your people's other (local) managers

When you run a remote team your team members may be 100% dedicated to you. It is just as likely that they will have another job and another boss as well. Either way they are likely to have a local population that they support, work with and identify with. This can be a cause of friction and challenge.

If your team member works X% for you and Y% for another team/boss/client:

■ Be aware of this: ask, investigate discuss it with the team member.
■ Remember it: when you are allocating tasks, take into account the team member's other work. When asking for updates, check that you aren't turning the team member's working day into one long progress report (it gets in the way of actually *doing* anything!). When you are trying to get in touch urgently, be aware that the team member may be engaged on work for their other boss. When you are running a team meeting don't overrun without considering the impact this will have on the team member's other job/boss/productivity.

■ Refer to it regularly: when you are talking with your individual team members.

■ Get in touch with their other bosses, introduce yourself, start a dialogue about the fact that you 'share a resource'.

■ Understand what your team member is doing for their other boss; what regular deadlines do they have to hit, what irregular pressures are they under?

■ Keep the other boss informed/updated about times of particular pressure on your shared people.

■ Work with the other boss to try to stagger deadlines so that not all the deliverables (regular or objective specific) are due at the same time or date.

■ Periodically thank the other boss for their support in helping your people work for you.

If your team member works 100% for you but is administered and logistically supported by the local 'country manager':

■ Make contact with the local manager and strike up a dialogue. Get to know about the local conditions under which your person works (you should already have done this as mentioned in Secrets 1.4 and 4.4, but it is worth getting a second opinion).

■ Let the local manager know that your team member enjoys your full support.

■ Ask the local manager to support your person fully and to keep you abreast of any issues in this matter.

■ Let your team member know that you are doing/have done this.
Periodically thank the local manager and his/her team for their support.

Don't leave your people split between two 'masters'; work with their other managers to help everyone achieve.

7.8

Think 'Goose'!

Some people think that running a virtual team is easier and less time consuming than running a co-located team. They are wrong! To avoid burnout, spread the load.

When geese migrate long distances, they fly in a '<' formation. Aerodynamically this makes it around 70% more energy efficient than flying in a single straight line. The goose at the front is the navigator, responsible for the direction and speed of the whole flock. If you are the team leader you are that goose. This goose is not benefiting from the energy saving advantage of the '<' formation. So, every so often, the lead goose drops to the back and the whole skein moves up one goose. This way everyone shares the burden of leadership for mutual advantage, and no one becomes totally dependent on a leader. You can share the load in several ways:

1 Ask people how they want to be communicated with by getting the team together to create the communication plan as discussed in Secret 7.1.

2 Give people the responsibility and confidence to contact you to ask for support and inform you about progress or problems.

3 Rotate the responsibility for running/chairing the regular team meetings.

Let's get back to those geese. As a skein of geese flies you can hear them constantly honking. That honking both tells the lead goose that the rest of the gang are still behind him or her. It also encourages that goose to keep going and maintain the present speed. That communication keeps the skein together, keeps it on schedule (Goose-Air Flight 147 to south-for-the-winter) and motivates the poor goose taking all the responsibility and working hardest.

You can get these benefits by:

- Offering constant encouragement to everyone in the team *as a team*.
- Offering regular and frequent encouragement to individual team members privately.
- Celebrating successes and achievements as and when they occur.
- Encouraging others to offer praise to their distant colleagues.
- Seeking feedback about your own successes and style.

If a goose is struggling and can't keep up, the whole skein will slow slightly to go at the pace of the slowest goose. They will do this unless this would endanger the whole skein. If this is the case, a few of the able-bodied geese will stay with the struggler to provide support and comradeship, forming a smaller skein until they can rejoin the main flock further along the route.

You can get similar benefits by getting your remote team to buddy-up in smaller groups for peer coaching, mentoring and a sense of camaraderie. Mix up the buddy groups; for instance, make up a group with a person from each continent or from different mother tongues. This way you'll get greater assistance than if you put all the English speakers in one group and all the Spanish speakers in another.

For a team, having a single 'Leader' is less important than having a constant culture of leadership.

7.9

Look for the signs that it is all going wrong

Out of sight can be out of mind. It is important, when running a remote team, to look out for signs that are symptomatic of a communications break-down. Some of these signs will be *visible* manifestations that something is wrong and others will be a distinct lack of anything.

Symptoms to look out for	Things missing that you might otherwise expect to see
a) People quitting. It is the most obvious sign that things are going wrong and it may be nothing to do with the communication per se. However, if the very first hint you get that a person is unhappy is their resignation, then the communication is broken as well. b) People 'going over to the other side'. If your people are getting 'Stockholm Syndrome' and identifying with their in-country colleagues rather than you and the rest of the team, this is a sure sign that your communications are broken and they are feeling isolated.	a) No communication except that which is mandated and work-related. b) No friendly chat at the beginning of virtual team meetings. c) No one knows what the weather is like where anyone else is; because they don't ask because they don't care. d) Forums or chat rooms you have set up have no traffic in them.

c) Your team is fragmenting into smaller cliques, especially of similar types of people. This suggests that your people are buddying-up (see Secret 7.8) in spite of the rest of the team rather than in support of it. d) Quality is suffering. This may be symptomatic of a failure to 'slow down to speed up'. Check it by increasing your communication.	

If you spot these signs start again to create a communication plan and to do all the other things mentioned in the secrets in this chapter. It is not too late to put it right.

Before you even start to think about bottom-line results, you need to spend a lot of time managing the communication of your remote team. It is worth investing this time!

Jargon buster

cc/bcc-carbon copy/blind carbon copy
The former means that everyone on the list sees the email AND knows who else has seen it. The latter means that although it may go to several people, none of them know who else is copied in.

Expatriate
A person who is living/working outside their native country.

F2F
Abbreviation for face to face.

GMT
Greenwich Mean Time (the time at the Greenwich Meridian, the datum line upon which time zones are based).

Lingua franca
A language systematically (as opposed to occasionally or casually) used to make communication possible between persons who do not share a native language.

Phatic communication
Those elements of a communication whose only function is to perform a social task, as opposed to conveying information; for example the 'How are you?', 'I hope you are having a good day' openers.

VOIP
Voice Over Internet Protocol; using the Internet to have a conversation.